UPCYCLING

20 Creative Projects Made
from Reclaimed Materials

UPCYCLING

20 Creative Projects Made from Reclaimed Materials

Max McMurdo
Photography by Simon Brown

jacqui small

First published in 2016 by
Jacqui Small LLP
74–77 White Lion Street
London N1 9PF

Publisher: Jacqui Small
Senior Commissioning Editor: Eszter Karpati
Managing Editor: Emma Heyworth-Dunn
Design and Art Direction: Rachel Cross
Editor: Sian Parkhouse
Photographer: Simon Brown
Illustration: Max McMurdo
Stylist: Caroline Davis
Production: Maeve Healy

The publisher and author would like to thank Home Barn for the loan
of vintage props.
www.homebarnshop.co.uk

The author has made every attempt to draw attention to safety precautions, but
it is the reader's responsibility to ensure safe working practices while carrying out
techniques outlined in this book.

ISBN: 978 1 91025 447 9

A catalogue record for this book is available from the British Library.

2018 2017 2016
10 9 8 7 6 5 4 3 2 1

Printed in China

Quarto is the authority on a wide range of topics.
Quarto educates, entertains and enriches the lives of
our readers — enthusiasts and lovers of hands-on living.
www.QuartoKnows.com

CONTENTS

FURNITURE 16

STORAGE & DISPLAY 60

LIGHTING & ACCESSORIES 88

TOOLS & TECHNIQUES 126

WHAT ON EARTH IS UPCYCLING?

The term 'upcycling' is actually relatively new, but it was initially used in the 1990s in Germany. Before its appearance I was simply referred to as a bit of a Womble who could be found rummaging in skips (dumpsters) before designing, cutting, sanding and generally pimping my finds to sell, as statement pieces. The key part of the word 'upcycling' is UP — unlike recycling, which takes a material backwards in the chain to its original properties, upcycling adds value to the item through clever design to make it more desirable, financially, aesthetically and emotionally.

Some people assume that the main reason for upcycling is purely financial. It's just a load of old scrap, right — so it must be cheap? Unfortunately, not always. Once you include a professional upcycler's overheads, such as workshop rent, rates, insurance, tools and other costs, plus labour rates for a skilled designer and craftspeople, what you get is a hand-crafted, unique piece of design that should last a lifetime and possibly go up in value — not a bargain. I for one think the fact that you are repurposing an item and taking it out of context in a playful manner is the main focus.

Inspiring others to get hands-on and make stuff themselves is also important, as is the positive environmental impact. If after all these positive attributes you also save some money, then that's a terrific bonus.

It all gets a bit confusing, but all of the terms below can refer to or include upcycling:

- Repurposed
- Shabby chic
- Reclaimed
- Salvaged
- Remade
- Preloved
- Reinvented

The list goes on, but ultimately if the items used in the design have performed another function or served a previous life then we are doing our bit and creating thought-provoking designs to inspire others along the way.

WHY NOT JUST BUY NEW?

That's a very good question. We are a generation of consumers: gone are the post-war times of make do and mend. New items are cheap, delivery is free and fashion changes so fast we don't invest in good-quality pieces of furniture to be handed down to our children — it's easier to just buy a new item of flat-pack chipboard every couple of years.

The reality is, however, that you get what you pay for, and these items usually do not last. Whereas if you were to invest in a solid piece of furniture from the 1950s or '60s it is likely to be so well made that it will probably outlive you! Tastes do change, but if the tone of the wood becomes dated, for example, rather than throwing an item out, could you sand and stain it, paint it or even modify it structurally?

It's also actually very short-sighted to buy these poor-quality, quick-fashion items. The profit margins are so small that the manufacturers don't tend to be around for long, the items are not designed to be repaired and you would probably struggle to find another item in the range a few years later as the design has already been superseded. Good design has longevity, both structurally and also aesthetically.

Another benefit of upcycling is that the item you create is unique; it represents you and your tastes. When guests come round for dinner they will ask you about it — it's a feature piece and a talking point.

Hopefully creating your own items will be far more enjoyable than simply buying them, too — and what's more the whole process can be educational. Even when you've been upcycling for years, as we have in the **reestore ltd** workshop, you still discover something new most days, whether it's how a certain material reacts when you cut it or which tool to use to cut a certain component. It's that experience of problem-solving that makes design so enjoyable for me.

Upcycling can involve different crafts and industrial processes. From taking old furniture and reinventing it with paint, to using reclaimed deckchair fabric and boat sails to make bags, people are upcycling everything these days.

THE IMPORTANCE OF GOOD DESIGN

Upcycling is more than just a current fashion statement. We have been cleverly reusing and working with salvaged materials for years. What's more, I'm keen to encourage good design as an essential part of the upcycling process. I'm not a huge fan of just sticking a clock mechanism or light bulb into an old object — good upcycling combines different materials and textures and references various genres and styles. It is moreover an opportunity to be thought-provoking and playful with design.

In our studio we often start a project with a blank piece of paper, as you would in more traditional design practices. We consider issues such as packaging, assembly, retailers' margins and sourcing materials as well as, of course, the aesthetics and functionality of the product. Only then do we pick up the material and have a good play with it, and sample various techniques and finishes. Upcycling is at times far from scientific. When working with a material for the first time it's almost impossible to predict how it will react, for example,

to cutting, folding, painting and other techniques. Who knew that when you cut a shipping container into 25 parts to carry it down a small alleyway to weld it all back together again that it would grow by 10cm (4in) due to each corrugation being produced under tension?

This of course is taking upcycling to a professional level. You may just fancy having a play. You might have an old family heirloom lying around that you don't really like, but you just can't bring yourself to throw away. With a bit of love, a lick of paint, perhaps some wallpaper or fabric and a day in the garden with a cuppa to keep you going, you might just fall in love with the item.

Whether you're spending an hour refurbishing an old chair, printing onto a plate, cutting the sleeves off a sweater or making a house out of a shipping container, it's all upcycling. You are adding value to an item of junk that would probably otherwise be discarded. And my favourite bit about upcycling is anyone can do it: young, old, rich, poor, beginner or expert!

There are some designs I've developed and created for my TV work that I would probably never have produced otherwise, either because they are not commercially viable to make as a one-off, or I didn't have the time or space. Take for example the Airbus a320 we upcycled for Channel 4's *Supersized Salvage* — what an incredible opportunity that was to cut up and play with an actual full-sized aeroplane!

In my very own shipping container houseboat as a space-saving device I designed the bathroom and kitchen to share a sink (see page 5). I then had to devise a tap (faucet) that tilted so it could be used from either side. Made out of a piece of aluminium scaffold pole and a riveted brown leather belt, it is the perfect combination of high-end design and reclaimed materials.

One of my earliest pieces was this sofa produced from a cast-iron roll-top bathtub. Over 20 hours of cutting, sanding, filing and upholstery goes into creating a finish that is often better than when it left the factory!

SOURCING GOOD MATERIALS

When it comes to finding materials for your projects there are really no rules. I thoroughly enjoy rooting around skips (dumpsters), attending auctions and rummaging through charity shops (thrift stores) but that is just me being weird I guess!

When I started out I used to find the waste items first and let them dictate the basic design in terms of proportions and aesthetics. More recently, however, I have found that I am given a brief by a client and I design the functionality and size of the item first, then select the materials to suit. It doesn't matter which way you work and you may find you actually switch between the two methods, depending on the project.

These are some of the things you need to think about:

SIZE – When designing your item the overall size of the raw materials can be important in a number of ways: space available in your work area, transport and ensuring you can get it in and out of buildings. My first design, a shopping trolley (cart) chair, didn't fit through a standard household door!

PRICE – We would all love to work with titanium and stainless steel but these materials can be costly, even second-hand. It is easy to get carried away in the thrill of the hunt so set yourself a budget: consider what you can afford but also the likely value of the finished piece, and try to use a suitable material that fits that price point.

AVAILABILITY – Searches can take you far and wide. We recently produced 300 bathtub chairs, which involved getting our hands on 150 cast-iron roll-top bathtubs, each one in a different location. We had to search every online auction house, scrapyard and online small ads listing we could find. Carrying them down narrow staircases, loading vans, then unloading and manhandling at our workshop was a nightmare!

FINISHES – Does the item of waste you have chosen require additional finishing once you have worked on it? Specialist finishes such as painting, lacquering and plating can be time consuming and costly, and need to be factored into your plans.

STYLE – Just because you are upcycling doesn't mean you cannot follow trends and be stylish. Right now the industrial look is very popular. For an original effect try combining complementary materials, such as warm rustic wood with cold contemporary glass or concrete.

JOINING MATERIALS – Something I find when I visit schools is that children have the most wild imaginations and inventive ideas, but never consider how to join items together – the world for children is stuck together with PVA glue and paperclips! When upcycling you need to be constantly thinking about how to join different materials. I prefer structural and mechanical fixings like nuts and bolts and screws, which also allow for flat-pack shipping and recycling after use. (See Fixing & Joining pages 138–41, for a rundown on lots of options.)

ULTIMATELY finding all of these items and dreaming up ideas of what they could become is incredibly fun and allows you to be almost childlike as there are no hard and fast rules. Go crazy and be brave.

There is something about furniture that makes the designer in me very happy. I don't have any specific qualifications in furniture design or manufacture — in fact, my degree is in general product design and my commercial experience in automotive design — but furniture design is a great challenge because it poses so many questions…

Is it beautiful, does it look balanced, does it play with the viewer? Does it appear delicate and cantilevered or look robust and structural? Does the item look too cold and clinical or maybe too fluffy and frilly? Does it have character? Does it tell a story? Would your average couple both like to have it in their home?

Then you have to consider the functionality. Is it comfortable, durable and does it serve its specified purpose? There is no point creating a chair that you cannot sit on or a table with a surface that can't hold items! If positioned in a public space, is it durable enough to stand up to children (and some adults) jumping all over it?

Then there are the separate issues if you wish to sell your work. Does it need to be tested? Does it have to be fire retardant? Does the client want them all the same or unique? How do you send the items out — do they need bespoke packaging? Does the customer need instructions on how to install the design or keep it in good condition? I've even been asked to design dining chairs for a restaurant that are only comfortable for an hour or so, to encourage people to finish dining within a set time, to fit in a second sitting to increase earnings!

Furniture reveals so much about someone. It's the first thing you see when you enter their house. It's how a person expresses themselves in a very personal way, and even if we don't do it intentionally it's how we judge them and their taste.

Please don't think for one second I am suggesting we all fill our homes with purely our upcycled creations. Even I don't have a home of entirely upcycled furniture and I live in a converted shipping container! I prefer a nice eclectic mix of quality second-hand items (I'm a huge fan of mid-century design) combined with a few newer items and a selection of stand-out upcycled feature pieces.

PALLET-WOOD UPHOLSTERED STOOL

This is a great project for amateur upcyclers as it involves lots of different techniques for you to experiment with — such as taking a pallet apart and adding upholstery — that can be used in lots of other projects.

Forgive me if I go on a bit in this book about pallets but I LOVE THEM! If you bought new timber and tried to give it a lovely distressed look it would take hours — pallets already look like this and are free. They are currently cluttering up industrial estates all over the world.

I think the trick with lots of junk items, but especially pallets, is to design your creation around the material. You can get large pallets with 2m (14 feet) long pieces of wood, but salvaging them intact can be tricky. I prefer to measure between the fixing points and use those dimensions in the design — so this storage box is perfect, measuring roughly 50cm (20in) wide by 30cm (12in) deep and 30cm (12in) tall. The construction is similar to an old wine or fruit crate.

ITEMS TO SOURCE:
- *Pallet*
- *Wood offcuts for framework*
- *Salvaged plywood for lid*
- *Upholstery foam*
- *Fire-retardant lining fabric*
- *Fabric*

MGW
Tare
Payload
kg 67200 lb
3780 kg 8330 lb
26700 kg 58870 lb
6E SeaCo
SRL.
Bridgetown,
Barbados

1. CUT TIMBER

Mark out the lengths of timber you require on the pallet (see How to take apart a wooden pallet, page 132). Create your stool to suit the dimensions of your pallet — you should easily have enough timber to create at least one crate, if not two. Cut 6 long lengths for the front, back and base, 4 medium for the sides and 2 short ones for the lid locaters. Lay the front sections out on your bench, leaving a gap, to determine the height of your uprights. Mark out and cut 4 square uprights to this height (although they protrude at the bottom to create the feet they are recessed at the top). Cut 2 square base pieces.

2. ASSEMBLE STOOL

Mark and pre-drill all the holes. This is the part of the process that takes a bit of time but it's worth getting right: the pilot holes and countersinking ensure the wood doesn't split as you are screwing it together. There is nothing worse than spending all that time cutting, sanding and waxing, then ruining the wood at the last stage. Partially screw any screws partway in while you have the item separate, and assemble each side flat on the bench to ensure it's flat and square. I use the corner of the workbench to keep things at right angles.

TIP: Trying to create fine tolerances and a perfect fit is almost impossible when working with reclaimed materials. A small overhang on the lid of about 10mm ($^3/_8$in) disguises the edge a little and also creates a nice lip to lift the lid.

3. CONSTRUCT LID

Mark out the lid on the plywood, curving the corners. Cut out. Draw around the wood on the foam, adding 5mm (¼in) all round. Cut with an electric carving knife (see Upholstery, pages 134–5). Cut lining fabric 10cm (4in) bigger all round.

4. STAPLE FABRIC COVER

Starting at the centres of each side, pull the lining fabric taut and staple into the wood. Work out from the centres of the sides to each corner. Cut out your fabric 10cm (4in) bigger all round and repeat the process.

5. FIX SUPPORT POSTS

Trim away any excess fabric. You can make the underside neater with a fabric cover, folded under all round. Then screw on the 2 wooden under-lid locators.

Hey presto, a stunning yet relatively simple upholstered storage crate and stool.

6. ADD SEAT/LID

BICYCLE-SADDLE STOOL

Although this design looks quite complex and scary, it actually involves a relatively simple process and allows you to reinvent a bicycle that would otherwise be scrapped. This bike actually belonged to my late father, and I had kept it for sentimental reasons. Transforming it into a stool has allowed me to enjoy it for longer, and keep it in everyday use, rather than leaving it to collect cobwebs in the garage.

ITEMS TO SOURCE:
- *Old bicycle*
- *Separate saddle*

1. FIND YOUR BIKE

Source a scrapped adult's bike. It will more than likely have a rubbish saddle, so try to source a sprung leather vintage one separately if you can.

2. STRIP IT DOWN

You need to remove all unnecessary bits from the bike frame. Remove the seat first (and retain it if you are going to reuse it). Move on to the handle bars, then remove the guards, brakes, the rear and front wheels and the pedals.

TIP: Old mechanical parts might be difficult to take apart. Lubricate well the day before with penetrating oil. If parts are still stubborn heat them with a blow torch.

3. CUT INTO FRAME

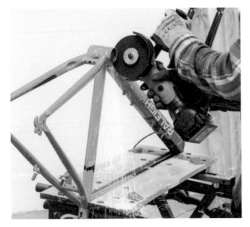

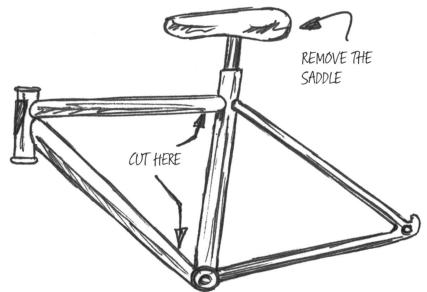

REMOVE THE SADDLE

CUT HERE

Cut away the back wheel mount triangular section using a cutting disc on a grinder. You could use a hacksaw, but it will take longer. (See sketch to know where to make your cuts.)

4. OPEN UP FRAME

Use a car trolley (floor) jack to press the frame apart to create an even pyramid. Cut away any bits sticking out of the main frame.

5. SAND

Sand the cut edges to make sure they are smooth, then sand over the entire frame to give a distressed feel and add texture.

6. ADD SEAT

Attach the sprung saddle, adjusting the height for comfort, and enjoy.

TIP: *Sparks fly! Wear goggles and gloves when you cut metal, and stay clear of flammable materials.*

SCAFFOLD-POLE COFFEE TABLE

In its proper environment scaffolding is designed to be put flat on a truck and assembled around random-sized and shaped buildings, so it has to be pretty easy to assemble and adaptable. Another good thing for upcyclers is that this stuff gets abused on building sites and the poles get dented and run over a lot. Scaffolders do sometimes trim them down or try to straighten the poles out, but when they get too short they are useless and get dumped in the yard — if you pay your local scaffolding company a visit with some cash in your pocket you'll be surprised with what you leave with!

We produce all sorts of things from scaffolding. The angled frame on this design, topped with glass cut to your desired shape and size, is inspired by the coffee tables produced by American designer Isamu Noguchi.

ITEMS TO SOURCE:
- *Scaffold poles*
- *Plastic end caps*
- *Scaffold elbow joints*
- *Glass — size and shape to order*
- *Rubber glass protector pads*

1. MEASURE POLES

Decide on the height and width of your table — this will dictate the lengths of pole you need. Measure and mark the 5 lengths required.

2. CUT TO LENGTH

Place each scaffold pole securely in a clamp and cut to length using a cutting disc on a grinder. Alternatively, you could use a hacksaw but, as I mentioned before, it will take longer. Always remember to wear protective goggles and gloves.

3. SMOOTH ENDS

Use a half-round metal file to smooth any sharp edges on the cut ends.

4. STOP ENDS

Seal one end of both the outer legs with plastic caps.

APPLY SELF-ADHESIVE RUBBER GLASS PROTECTORS

5. ASSEMBLE FRAME

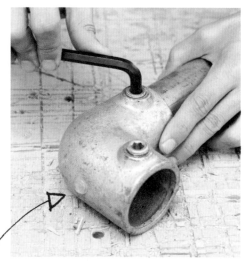

Slot the poles into the elbow joints and use an Allen key (hex wrench) to loosely secure.

6. ADJUST SHAPE

Stand the frame up to make sure you have it in the desired position before finally tightening. Use a spirit level spanning the top in different directions to make sure the top is flat.

8. ADD GLASS TOP

7. MAKING YOUR TEMPLATE

Make a template for the glass top using plywood or thick rigid card. Take this to your glass shop for them to produce the glass top. Use 12mm (1/2in) toughened glass with polished edges. Use protector pads to cushion the glass; its weight will keep it firmly in place.

DRAW BETWEEN POINTS WITH RULER

TO CREATE CURVED CORNERS DRAW AROUND PLATES, MUGS OR OTHER CROCKERY

THREE-CHAIR BENCH

Charity and thrift shops and furniture banks across the country are inundated with sets of three dining chairs and it fascinates me! Basically, in the olden days everyone wanted a set of four identical dining chairs around a matching dining table. Times have changed, however, and I personally think it's far more creative and eye-catching to have four or six differently styled chairs around an old farmhouse table. This means it is not only cheaper to buy them in the first place but easier to replace one if it gets damaged. It also creates a lovely eclectic look, with complementary and contrasting colours, textures and fabrics.

Back to the charity shop! What you'll find is that one of the set of four has been damaged or broken beyond repair, so the entire set has been thrown out or donated. Three chairs are no longer a full set and therefore almost unsaleable in a furniture bank or charity shop where the majority of shoppers tend to have a more conservative outlook towards interior design. Their loss is clearly our gain and an upcycler's dream — once you have three chairs you can get designing. The main concept behind this idea is that you end up with the three chairs side by side with one large cushion spanning the separate chairs.

ITEMS TO SOURCE:
- *3 chairs*
- *Plywood at least 18mm ($^3/_4$in) thick*
- *Upholstery foam*
- *Fabric*
- *Fire-retardant lining fabric*

1. SELECT YOUR STYLE

Do you want all the chairs to match or each chair to be a different colour? I'm leaving mine white and will distress them.

2. STRIP OUT SEATS

Remove any existing upholstered seat pads. You might have to use a flat-head screwdriver or, depending on the age and style of the chairs, they will have simple tabs that rotate and release the seat pads.

3. MEASURE NEW SEAT

Place the chairs side by side, ensuring they are square to each other, and measure the size of your new bench seat, allowing it to hang over both sides and the front by 10–18mm ($^3/_8$–$^3/_4$in). Use a thick piece of wood to create the new base. An offcut of plywood would do, or perhaps 2 scaffold boards. Just make sure it is at least 18mm ($^3/_4$in) thick, as this is the main structural element holding the entire bench together.

4. SAND

If like me you want a distressed finish, sand the paintwork on each chair. Concentrate on edges and areas of high usage to replicate natural wear and tear and reveal the wood or other paint colours below.

6. CUT CURVES

Use a jigsaw to cut out the shape. Jigsaws are fantastic for cutting curves but not so great for straight lines. Sand the cut edges.

5. SHAPE BENCH

Place the piece of wood over the chairs and mark up the curved edges, using the shapes of the chairs as your guide.

7. MARK FOAM

Place the wood on your upholstery foam and draw around it by about 5mm (½in) bigger all round – angling the nib slightly plus the thickness of the pen should do it.

8. CUT FOAM

Cut out the foam along the outline using a sharp kitchen carving or bread knife. A standard electric carving knife also works well for this (see Upholstery, pages 134–5).

9. ATTACH LINING FABRIC

Cut a piece of fire-retardant lining fabric 10cm (4in) bigger all round than the foam. This is a safety feature but also prevents the upholstery fabric from rubbing against the foam. Starting with the centre of each side, pull the fabric up with one hand to create tension, then staple it into the wood about 5cm (2in) from the edge. Continue stapling from the centre to the corners along each side. You can either smooth the creases out and curve it round the corners or fold them into a box pleat similar to the way you might make a hospital bed.

10. ATTACH UPHOLSTERY FABRIC

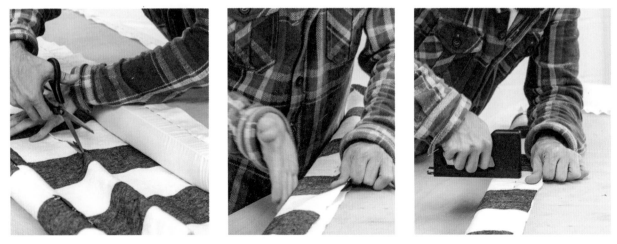

Lay the lined bench seat over your chosen seat fabric and cut to size, adding 10cm (4in) all round. Staple in place on the underside. Again, start in the centre of the sides. Turn over to check the fabric looks good from the other side. Finish stapling, by working out to the corners, pulling the fabric smooth and taut over the foam as you go.

11. FIX SEAT IN PLACE

Place the upholstered seat across the 3 chairs. Screw it into place from underneath, upwards through the chairs (hopefully reusing the existing holes in the chairs if possible). Your new bench is now secure.

WHEELBARROW CHAIR

This is one of my favourite designs, mainly because builders have been sitting in upturned wheelbarrows for years! They of course don't upholster them, but they do utilize the natural ergonomics the wheelbarrow pan provides. The other reason I love this design is that you can actually save an old office chair from the skip at the same time as repurposing the wheelbarrow pan.

I personally love an old rusty barrow with a flat tyre and wonky wheel — they have a certain rustic charm! Alternatively, go for a more playful plastic — this final design is very reminiscent of the egg and ball chairs from the 1960s and '70s.

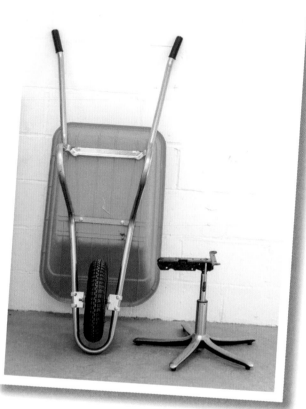

ITEMS TO SOURCE:
- *Wheelbarrow*
- *Office chair base*
- *Plywood for seat and back*
- *Wood offcuts for wedges*
- *Upholstery foam*
- *Artificial grass*

1. DISMANTLE WHEELBARROW

Firstly, you will need to find the donor wheelbarrow. Carefully separate the pan from the framework; usually this is just held together with 4 bolts — they may be a bit rusty from years of water collection so a little squirt of spray penetrating oil and a light tap with the hammer will possibly help.

2. POSITION NEW LEGS

Remove the seat from an old office chair, saving the swivel leg base. Position it on the bottom of the barrow pan. Remember this doesn't just have to be structurally balanced, it also needs to look right visually, so ask a friend to hold it in place or use some clamps so you can stand back to judge whether it looks nice and stable.

Mark points in the wheelbarrow through the existing holes in the metal chair base. Drill through using a metal drill bit. Fit nuts and bolts to secure the base, not forgetting washers both sides of the plastic. Tighten each one securely.

3. ATTACH CHAIR BASE

4. MEASURE SEAT AND BACK SECTIONS

Measure the back and seat areas to find out the height and width of the pieces you need for the upholstery. Depending on the shape of your wheelbarrow, you might need to taper the front of the seat section to make it wider than the back.

5. MARK OUT

6. CUT WOOD

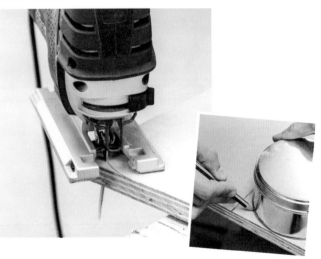

Transfer your measurements onto your wood. For the corners, rather than a freehand curve, draw round something like a tin of paint to ensure all the shapes are consistent. Cut around the shapes using a jigsaw, then sand.

7. ANGLE BACK PIECE

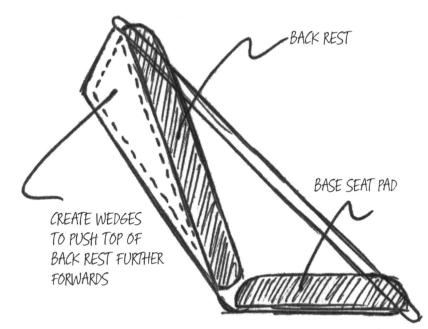

BACK REST

BASE SEAT PAD

CREATE WEDGES
TO PUSH TOP OF
BACK REST FURTHER
FORWARDS

8. FIX SUPPORT WEDGES

To position the chair back at a comfortable
angle you will probably need to support it.
Find the correct angle, then create a pair
of wedges from any old scrap of wood.
Screw the wedges to the back section.

9. MARK OUT SHAPES AND CUT FOAM

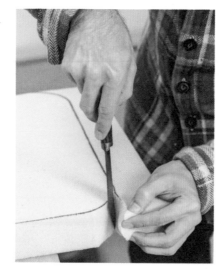

Use the wooden back rest as a template to draw around on the foam, making it slightly bigger all round by about 5mm ($^1/_4$in). Do the same for the base. You can use a kitchen knife to cut out the shapes, or see Upholstery, pages 134–5 for other cutting methods.

TIP: Hang the foam over the edge of the bench to make cutting easier.

10. UPHOLSTERING THE CUSHIONS

Cut out the grass with a sharp knife (box cutter) using the foam as a template, and adding 10cm (4in) extra all round. You can use spray glue to attach the wood to the foam to stop it slipping. Staple the fabric to the wood. Start in the centre of each side, then work out to the corners, folding and tucking neatly.

11. ATTACH SEAT AND BACK PADS

Screw the upholstered pieces to the wheelbarrow pan. If possible, use the holes left when you removed the wheelbarrow framework – if not you will need to pre-drill new holes. Remember to add washers to prevent the screw pulling through.

INDUSTRIAL-STYLE COFFEE TABLE

I'm a huge fan of the industrial look but sometimes it can be a little bit stark and lacks a certain cosiness and warmth. I believe the key to creating a successful industrial look in your home is to combine the harsher metal surfaces with warmer wood tones. This coffee table proves that upcycling can be subtle. An engine table doesn't need to just be a piece of glass placed on an entire engine block – with this design we utilize the iconic con rods from the engine to form the legs of the wooden table top and add a touch of retro nostalgic fun with the addition of the naturally patinated Meccano wheels.

ITEMS TO SOURCE:
* *Scaffold boards*
* *Connecting rods (con rods) from a car engine*
* *Metal wheels*

1. CLEAN METALWORK

Brush your con rods with paint thinner to remove all traces of engine grease. You might need to repeat this, or soak overnight if they are especially dirty.

2. CUT AND MEASURE WOOD

Decide how long you want your table to be, then measure and cut the scaffold boards to size. The width will be dictated by how many boards you choose to place alongside each other. Cut 2 braces with angled ends, a single piece for the lower shelf and a small offcut for the foot underneath. Wax all wood.

3. FIX BRACKETS

To assemble the table top, screw the boards together, using a sash clamp to ensure a tight fit. Screw the 2 braces on the underside, 5cm (2in) in from the outer short edges.

IF YOU CAN, FIX 4 SCREWS IN EACH BOARD TO PREVENT TWISTING

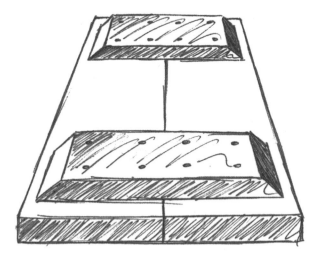

4. FIT CON RODS AND LOWER SHELF

Using the existing holes in the con rods, screw them onto the underside of the braces to form the legs. Offer up the shelf to the con rods and mark the hole positions with a pencil. Screw through the holes of the con rods into the sides of the timber, using screws and metal washers on one end and screws and metal wheels on the other.

5. BALANCE WHEELS

Add a small offcut as a foot under the set of con rods without the metal wheels to accommodate the height of the wheels at the other end.

6. ADD HANDLE

Finally, add a handle formed from the upper portion of one of the con rods, screwing it into place on top of the table through the existing holes.

SCAFFOLD-BOARD KITCHEN TABLE

I'm a huge fan of flat-pack and modular furniture — these scaffold fixings allow you to create your own. With just the twist of an Allen key (hex wrench) you can remove the legs of this table, offering flexibility and convenient storage. You could even take it outside to use as an impromptu picnic table. Scaffolding is designed to support the weight of a team of workers, so it lends itself particularly to table construction. The industrial aesthetic contrasts the rustic boards with the cool metal poles for a robust yet stylish dining solution.

ITEMS TO SOURCE:
- *Scaffold boards*
- *Scaffold board or plywood for braces*
- *Scaffold poles*
- *Scaffold mounts*
- *Plastic end caps*

1. MEASURE, MARK AND CUT WOOD

Decide on the length of the scaffold boards you want for your table top. Use enough boards lined up next to each other to give you the width you want. Cut the boards square at a 90° angle, using the handle on your handsaw as your guide. Cut 2 braces with a 45° angled edge all round using a mitre saw. Sand ready for assembly.

2. ASSEMBLE TABLE TOP

To create the table top attach the individual boards together by screwing from the underside through the bevelled braces using countersunk screws. Alternatively, you can brace the top with a single sheet of plywood cut slightly smaller than the boards.

3. CUT POLES

Decide on the height for the legs (the standard height for a table is 70–80 cm/28–32in from the top surface to the floor), then cut the poles using the cutting disc on an angle grinder. Secure the poles in a vice, and wear goggles.

4. ATTACH SCAFFOLD MOUNTS

Decide where to place the scaffold fixings, considering the most comfortable seating position of the users and the overall stability of the table. Drill pilot holes as a guide, then screw the scaffold mounts in position. Place a pole in each mount and secure with an Allen key (hex wrench). Add plastic end caps to prevent the cut ends of the poles scratching the flooring.

YOUR VERY OWN PORTABLE 'FLAT-PACK' TABLE, READY TO GO.

TIP: Angling the sides of the braces at 45° allows you to put your legs under the table comfortably, without bumping into sharp edges.

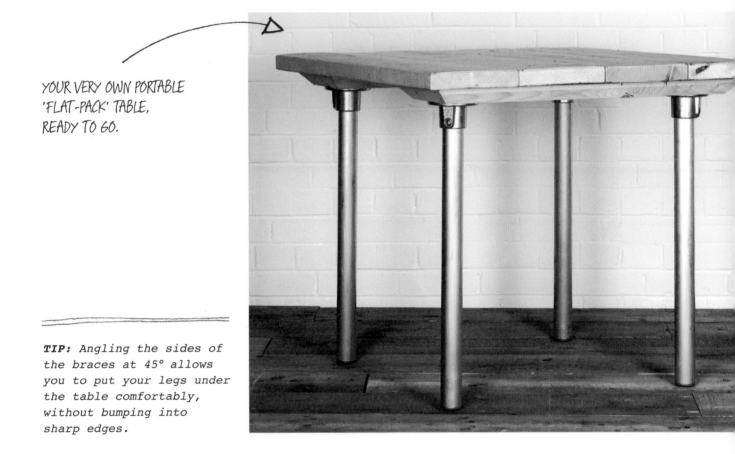

WASHING-MACHINE DRUM ILLUMINATED SIDE TABLE

The wash-drum table was the second item I ever made from junk. I'd seen the drums used in gardens as fire pits but I wanted to create something spectacular, modern and high-end that wouldn't look out of place in a contemporary penthouse apartment. The integrated light bulb creates beautiful streams of light through the original holes and a warm ambient glow through the frosted-glass top.

ITEMS TO SOURCE:
- *Old drum from a washing machine*
- *Light fitting and bulb*
- *Cable and switch*
- *Rubber grommet*
- *Metal strip for mount for bulb*
- *Metal threaded rods*
- *Glass — size and shape to order*

1. CLEAN UP DRUM

If the drum has built up a covering of limescale from being used in a hard water area, remove this with a proprietary scale-removing product and lots of scrubbing. A high shine will really contribute to the look of the finished table. To achieve this use an abrasive cleaner such as T-Cut and a lint-free soft cloth. Keep buffing until you have the effect you want.

TIP: *Abrasive cleaning products designed for removing scratches from car paintwork are readily available and do a great job transforming old metalwork into a super-shiny state.*

2. DRILL HOLE FOR CABLE

Turn the drum upside down and drill a hole through the centre to feed the cable through. Fit a rubber grommet to the hole to protect the cable from the sharp metal edge.

GROMMET PROTECTS WIRE FROM SHARP METAL EDGE ON DRUM

3. MAKE LAMP SUPPORT

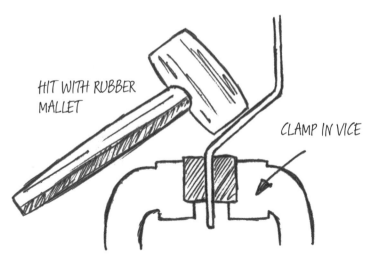

HIT WITH RUBBER MALLET

CLAMP IN VICE

To mount the lamp holder at a good height inside the drum simply fold a piece of thin metal using a vice. Alternatively, you could just use an old tin can or even repurpose a lampshade fitting.

Cut a hole to the right size for the fitting using a hole saw. Thread the cable through the grommet in the base of the drum and the lamp support.

4. FIT LAMP SUPPORT AND BULB

Position your lamp support within the drum. You can fix this in place using nuts and bolts. Fit a light bulb - energy saving of course! – and a plug.

5. MEASURE AND MARK RODS

To gauge the length of the 3 metal rods that support the glass top measure the height of the wash drum and add 7cm (3in).

6. CUT RODS

Cut each rod using a hacksaw or angle grinder. When you cut a threaded rod it usually needs to be filed afterwards to reshape the thread.

7. FIX RODS

Thread the rods through the existing holes in the drum that were originally used to suspend it in the washing machine. Fit a washer and domed nut to each rod to create the foot. Slide the rods into the holes from the base, then fit another washer and nut on the top of the drum to secure the rod in place.

TIP: When cutting anything with a thread, such as a screw or rod, you can also apply a nut before you cut it — then when you remove the nut it reshapes the thread.

8. PLACE GLASS ON TOP

Make a template for the glass top using plywood or thick rigid card, including marks to indicate the holes for the rods. Take this to your glass shop for them to produce the glass top. Order 8–12mm ($^3/_8$–$^1/_2$in) toughened glass with polished edges. Fit another nut with a metal washer, and a rubber washer on each rod, then carefully slide the glass into place on the rods. One last rubber washer and domed nut on the top of each rod and hey presto.

Storage units are not usually known for their quirkiness or beauty, but why not? Just because an item is practical doesn't mean it can't be great to look at and made out of innovative, reused materials. You've already seen some projects I made from scaffold boards and poles and here you can see how I made a feature of them in my kitchen storage.

I think designing a product that is required to hold other objects just adds to the challenge. Is there an innovative way to hold the item?

What are the dimensions and weights to consider? You'll notice a couple of my storage designs are free-standing and lean against a wall for support. With an increasing number of people renting as house prices around the world soar, we need to think about smarter, more flexible furniture that can be installed without permanent wall fixings, and which can possibly even pack flat for moving and delivery purposes.

Consider the fixings in your own designs. Do we really need to see screw heads? Are visible brackets necessary and will the areas in contact with the floor need to be soft and non-marking?

Having recently designed the storage in my upcycled shipping container houseboat, I even started analysing the items I store. Should they be locked away behind closed doors or should we celebrate the things we own and the brands we buy?

As Arts and Crafts designer William Morris famously put it: 'Have nothing in your homes that you do not know to be useful or believe to be beautiful.'

SKATEBOARD SHELF

This shelf makes such a great gift, especially if the item has some
sentimental value but is no longer useable for its original purpose.
I've created shelves from lots of items, but skateboards and snowboards
are perfect as they are usually mostly made from plywood. If you are
careful in your cutting you could make two complete shelves from one board,
using both sets of trucks and wheels. Most modern boards are brightly
decorated already, but if yours is an
old-school wooden one, you might need to
do a bit of sanding to tidy it up and
then apply some wax or paint to finish.
Or you could even add your own graffiti.

ITEMS TO SOURCE:
- *Old skateboard*
- *Metal brackets*

1. STRIP BOARD

The first thing to do is strip the board and remove all the trucks, wheels and bindings. Remember to put any nuts back onto the bolts and label anything with masking tape to make sure nothing gets lost.

2. MARK YOUR CUTTING LINE

Clamp the board to your bench firmly. Measure and mark out a cutting line halfway across the top surface of the board lengthways.

3. CUT BOARD

Once you have marked the bare board it's time to cut it in half lengthways. Cutting along the length of a material is known as ripping. It seems daunting, but once you get started as long as you take your time and let the saw do the work you'll be fine. Use the full length of the saw blade and press quite gently. When you get towards the end of the cut try to take the weight off.

TIP: Before you start check what the board is made from. For example, if it has a metal edge notch this out using a hacksaw before you start your lengthways cut.

4. MOUNT TRUCKS

The trucks already have 4 holes on a flat surface, which is ideal for wall mounting so we are going to utilize 2 simple small metal brackets to mount onto the underside of the board. You can buy brackets like this from hardware stores.

5. POSITION BRACKETS

Simply slide the brackets onto one of the trucks then bolt the whole assembly back together. Now mark the shelf through the holes in the brackets.

6. DRILL PILOT HOLES

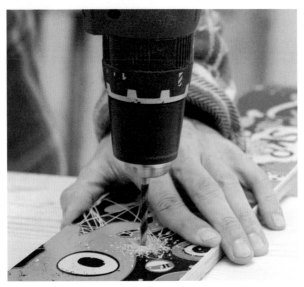

Drill holes slightly larger than the bolts. You may wish to countersink these from the top. Place your board on a flat even surface on top of waste wood to protect your worktop.

7. RE-ATTACH WHEELS

Bolt the brackets to the board. Bolt the wheels back in place and then you are ready to fix the board to the wall through the existing holes in the truck.

SPARK-PLUG KEY HOOKS

These coat hooks are a great gift for the car nut in your life. Their pride and joy sits in the garage and gets wheeled out at weekends for a wash but what do you buy them for Christmas or birthdays? Well why not ask them if you can have the old spark plugs next time the car gets serviced — they will still be in great condition and once cleaned look as good as new! The spark plug is, in my opinion, an object of intrinsic beauty. It has a porcelain jacket around a stainless steel body and once mounted on a distressed piece of wood it looks gorgeous. Pallet wood is perfect for this as it's strong, easy to work with and creates a warm, rustic look to complement the industrial metal and ceramic of the plugs.

ITEMS TO SOURCE:
* *Pallet wood*
* *Selection of old spark plugs*

1. CLEAN SPARK PLUGS

Give the spark plugs a good clean in methylated spirits or paint thinner to remove engine grease and grime.

2. MEASURE DIAMETER

To judge how large you need to make your holes in the board, measure the diameter of the spark plugs with a Vernier calliper (it is usually 16mm/^{1}/$_2$in but can vary). Select a drill bit 1–2mm (^{1}/$_{16}$in) smaller than your measurement so that the thread of the spark plugs taps into the wood — wood is softer than metal so will grip the thread firmly.

3. WORK OUT SPACING

Lay your spark plugs out on your piece of wood until you are happy with the spacing. Find and mark the centre point of the wood as your starting point and work out from there, however many spark plugs you are using. Odd numbers usually work better visually.

TIP: Utilizing a product's built-in fixing, such as the threads of these spark plugs, is better than retro fitting.

4. CONCEAL WALL FIXINGS

There is no point creating a lovely looking product and then spoiling it with visible screws when you come to fix the board to the wall. A neat trick is to hide the wall fixing within the holes for the spark plugs to conceal the screw heads. Drill through the outer 2 holes if possible.

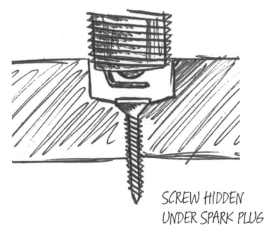

Drill pilot holes to stop the wood splitting. Then, using the drill bit you selected in step 2, add a piece of tape to indicate the required depth for the holes for the spark plugs and drill the required holes.

SCREW HIDDEN
UNDER SPARK PLUG

5. TEST SPARK PLUGS FIT

After you have drilled the holes sand your piece of wood and then wax, highlighting any areas of interest on the wood. I really like the driftwood effect of the broken edge on the bottom of this board. Give the spark plugs a test run to ensure they fit snugly before fixing the board to the wall through the empty holes. Insert the spark plugs to cover your fixings.

6. ATTACH TO WALL

LEAN-TO PALLET HERB PLANTER

Space is at a premium and gardens are getting smaller, yet we are encouraged to eat home-grown food. This is a simple yet stylish solution that allows you to grow your own herbs even if you live in a small rented property. Chalkboard paint is now available in almost any colour and allows you to personalize your planter. I've got one of these on my container houseboat and there is no better feeling than stepping out to pick freshly grown herbs — straight from your upcycled planter to your pot!

ITEMS TO SOURCE:
- Old pallet
- Other offcuts of pallet wood
- Heavy-duty plastic or rubble sacks
- Scaffold boards
- Chalkboard paint

1. CLEAN UP PALLET

Make any necessary repairs to the pallet. Bang in any sharp or protruding nails or pins and make sure the structure is sound.

2. MAKE TROUGHS

Measure, mark and cut pieces of pallet wood offcuts to form the bases of the troughs that will hold the plants. Drill pilot holes and then screw each piece into place, positioning them against the structure of the pallet. Try to fix into the thickest part of the pallet whenever possible.

3. LINE TROUGHS

You can either place plants in pots in the troughs or fill the troughs with compost and plant directly. If you want to do that you will need to line the troughs with tough plastic. Push the plastic into each trough and secure in place with a staple gun. Trim the edges neatly and make a few holes in the base for drainage so your plants don't get waterlogged.

TIP: Pallet wood is prone to splitting, unlike scaffolding board wood, which is closer grained, so always make a pilot hole before you screw into it.

4. MEASURE AND CUT SUPPORTS

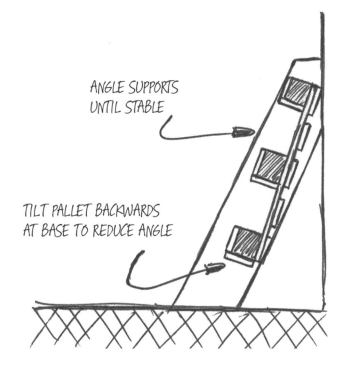

ANGLE SUPPORTS
UNTIL STABLE

TILT PALLET BACKWARDS
AT BASE TO REDUCE ANGLE

Measure and mark the scaffold boards for the side pieces. Tilt the pallet against the wall to judge the angle you need to cut from the scaffold board. Cut the angled ends.

5. SCREW TOGETHER

Screw the scaffold boards into the sides of the pallet, making sure you fix through the thick block section of the pallet for the most secure attachment.

6. PAINT FRONTS

Apply chalkboard paint to the fronts of the troughs for a finishing touch. You can decorate this how you like or use it to identify the plants. We added the names of our herbs.

SALVAGED DRAWER SHELVING UNIT

With more people renting than ever before, furniture that leans rather than being fixed to a wall is increasingly popular. This bookcase doubles up as a writing desk and is designed and built around a pair of salvaged drawers. The waxed and distressed scaffold boards are structurally solid and look beautiful alongside the repaired drawer fronts. Often an old chest of drawers will have some damage to the top surface or the carcass but the drawers themselves are usually in good structural condition.

ITEMS TO SOURCE:
- *Scaffold boards*
- *Old drawers*
- *Scaffold pole*
- *Scaffold mounts*

1. MARK ANGLES

Using a sliding bevel mark out the angles on the bottom and top of each upright so they will sit flat on the floor when the unit is leaning against the wall. (See sketch below.)

2. CUT WOOD

Use a handsaw or mitre saw to cut the angles. Measure, mark and cut scaffold board for the drawer housing and the shelf. Use your drawers as your starting point for the depth and then decide how wide you would like your unit to be. Wax all wood.

3. CONSTRUCT DRAWER HOUSING

Offer the drawer up to the side support to calculate the height. Assemble your pre-cut boards around the drawers for the housing.

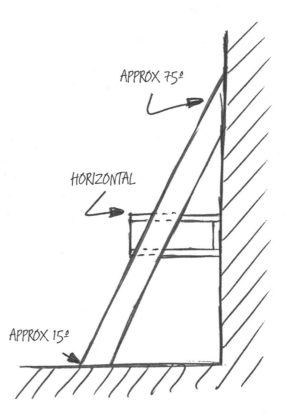

APPROX 75º

HORIZONTAL

APPROX 15º

4. ATTACH SCAFFOLD MOUNTS

Cut your scaffold pole to the same width as your shelf to form the top crossbar. This adds stability, gives an industrial edge and is useful hanging storage. Measure and mark where the scaffold mounts should be on the insides of the uprights and screw them in place.

5. PREPARE DRAWERS

If you want to paint your drawers, remove the handles first. Cutting around the handles would be fiddly and time-consuming. Sand down your surface. Two thin coats of paint give a much better finish than one thick coat. Replace the handles.

6. ASSEMBLE THE UNIT

Now you can put the unit together. Screw the drawer housing to the first of the 2 uprights. Fix the scaffolding pole into position before screwing the second upright to the drawer housing. Finally, screw the top shelf into place.

Slide the drawers into place — if they are sticking you can rub some beeswax along the bottom edges until they run smoothly. Then fill your new unit with your favourite books and files.

SHOPPING BASKET BATHROOM STORAGE

My first-ever design was a shopping trolley (cart) chair and ever since I've been wondering what to do with their little siblings — the humble and under-loved shopping basket. Recently we have seen increased popularity in warehouse-style living combined with industrial materials which has resulted in metal-caged storage units becoming must-have items. Why not produce your own unique bathroom storage by cutting and folding a shopping basket? Most supermarkets have mountains of discarded shopping baskets and trolleys (carts) at the back of the store — just ask the manager. You can also find them in vintage stores or listed on online auction sites.

ITEMS TO SOURCE:
* *Old discarded shopping basket*

1. MARK CUTTING LINES

Use a permanent marker pen to indicate where to make cuts for your shelves. You are going to fold your new shelf into place, so you only want cuts on two sides. That way you will not need to re-attach any sections and the shelf will have greater stability.

2. SECURE BASKET

Clamp the shopping basket to a workbench securely so you can work on it safely. You will need to move it around to get into some of the more awkward spots.

3. MAKE CUTS

CUT THROUGH THE HANDLES AND THEN UNHOOK

Cut according to your marks with a cutting disc on an angle grinder. You need long ends to form the loops to secure the shelf so cut each of the wires long enough to fold back on itself.

4. FORM SHELVES

Start to bend the shelves into position. This will create weaker points so try to maintain the structural integrity of the basket as much as possible. The wire should bend easily. But try not to force it or you could snap some of the thinner metal.

TIP: Don goggles and thick gloves to protect your eyes and hands from sharp edges and flying sparks.

5. WRAP

Use the ends of the wire to fix the shelves in their new positions. Where you can, loop around a junction of intersecting wires for more strength.

6. BEND

Use crocodile-nosed pliers to bend and secure the ends of the wires back on themselves firmly. Finally, file any sharp points until they are smooth.

LIGHTING & ACCESSORIES

Lights are incredibly powerful design tools. You can change the entire ambience of a room by simply changing a light. I am personally not a huge fan of hanging a large, obtrusive light bulb in the centre of the room — they can be very restrictive in the way they dictate the layout possibilities, as well as creating a harsh, uncontrollable central light source in the space. I much prefer free-standing lamps. They are flexible, portable and allow you to introduce new colours and materials into the room's palette. The other wonderful thing about lamps if you plan on selling your items is that people are like magpies — customers absolutely love anything that is shiny and lights up!

I never thought I'd have a favourite light bulb but the old-style filament bulbs are very much in fashion and I personally think they are gorgeous. What's even better is that now instead of having to decide between the stunning non-energy-efficient filament bulbs or energy-saving yet ugly LEDs, companies are now producing filament LEDs. You can only imagine my excitement when I first found these!

Please take care when wiring any lamps. It's generally only a question of tightening up screws but if in doubt please consult a qualified electrician.

The beauty of accessories and lights is that they make great gifts. Even your most design-conscious friends and family will be blown away if you give them a hand-crafted gift rather than something shop purchased. You could also try to make something sentimental or incorporate an upcycled item with emotional relevance.

CONDUIT-PIPEWORK CANDELABRA

There are so many designs you can create with electrical conduit piping. I love the fact that it used to be utilized as a cheap surface-mounted alternative to chasing out walls and hiding electrical cables. But now, with the industrial look being more popular than ever, conduit on display is a big thing! All the different components are available from an electrical wholesaler and cost very little.

This design is a very simple single bulb lamp with a couple of candles to add a cheeky playful twist, but as the fixings simply screw together you can adapt and tweak it to add your own touch. The only real manufacturing to speak of is if you need to cut the conduit pipe — you will need to file the end and retap the thread.

ITEMS TO SOURCE:
* *Assorted lengths and junctions of electrical metal conduit piping, including circular junction boxes and elbow joints*
* *Electric lamp holder, with switched electrical cable*
* *Thread adapter*

1. DECIDE ON YOUR DESIGN

Lay out your different components and find a shape that you are happy with. A circular junction box makes a great base and will allow the candelabra to stand upright, so make this your starting point. Then decide how many candle holders you want. You could of course keep it basic and not include any electrical light fitting, creating a design solely for candles, with 3 or 4 arms. You can see how my design was built up overleaf.

2. DRILL HOLE FOR THE CABLE

Drill a hole through the side of the circular junction box for the electrical cable to feed through. To insulate the hole insert a rubber grommet. This prevents the electrical cable being damaged by the sharp cut metal edges of the hole.

3. START ASSEMBLY

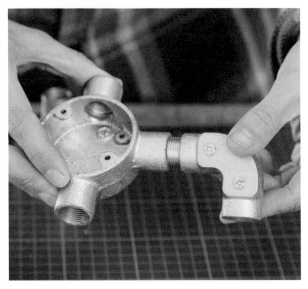

Connect together all the conduit components using the pre-threaded joins until you have your desired structure.

4. ADD LAMP HOLDER

Attach the lamp holder to the conduit at the top of the candelabra using a thread adapter.

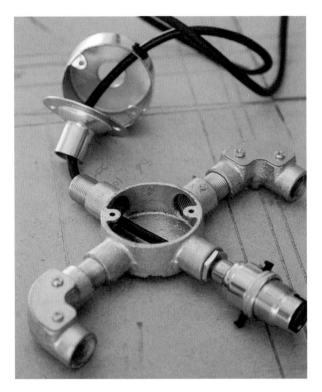

5. CONNECT CABLE

Connect one end of the electrical cable into the lamp holder. Pass the other end through the structure and out through the grommet in the base. Do up the remaining connections in the conduits. Attach a plug to the cable, add a bulb and some candles and you are ready to go!

TIP: Before you tighten every joint firmly do a test run to make sure the wiring works.

CARNIVAL LETTER LIGHTS

These beautiful illuminated letters have become very fashionable and endless varieties are available in shops and online. But they can be expensive, so why not make your own using an old pallet, some fairy lights and scraps of wood? You can create the initials of a loved one, write EAT on your dining room wall, position an **&** sign between two photos and make a great wedding gift. These carnival lights are a great example of how upcycling doesn't just have to be about finding some junk and doing something crafty with it — you can actually reverse the process by selecting an item you desire, then carefully designing and producing it from appropriate repurposed materials.

ITEMS TO SOURCE:
- *Wood for the backing board*
- *A string of LED lights with round bulbs*
- *Pallet wood*

1. FIND BACKING BOARD

Select a piece of relatively flat and thick timber for the backing board. You can cut away any damaged edges.

Measure and mark out the size of board you require, making sure your edges are perfectly square. Cut out using a handsaw, then sand the edges smooth.

2. MEASURE AND MARK

3. DECORATE

Draw on your chosen letter or letters. Mark out the outline in pencil then use a black marker pen. Add some vibrant colour using acrylic paint and allow to dry.

***TIP:** Use the internet to source some suitable fonts that give a carnival or circus feel. There are lots of free ones that you can print out and copy.*

4. POSITION LIGHTS

Work out the spacing for the lights, according to how many you have on your string and how they work best with the design of your letter(s). Keep the spacing even for the best effect — too many will detract from the lettering rather than enhance it. Mark with a pencil. You can reuse old Christmas lights, or choose the ones that have globe-shaped bulbs for an authentic carnival look.

5. ROUT HOLES

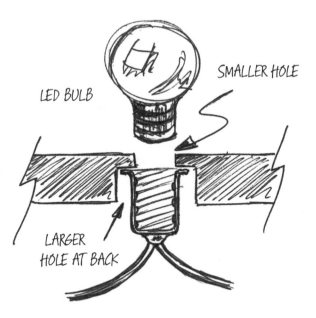

LED BULB

SMALLER HOLE

LARGER HOLE AT BACK

Using a router and working from the front create the smaller holes for the bulb stems. Then turn the board over and rout larger holes on the back, this time routing out three-quarters of the thickness of the backing board (see sketch). This will create a lipped edge for the bulb to sit in.

6. MEASURE AND CUT FRAME

Using old pallet wood, cut the pieces for the frame. Take your measurements from the backing board, factoring in a 45° angle at each of the mitred corners. Cut using a mitre saw, or a handsaw and mitre block.

TIP: You could use a butt joint for a frame but a 45°-angle mitre joint gives a more professional finish.

7. CONSTRUCT FRAME

Rest the backing board face down on a book or some offcuts of wood so that it is lifted off the bench. This will enable you to attach the frame pieces at the right depth, allowing space for the bulbs to sit within the finished frame rather than proud of it. Nail the first side in place.

Fit the next side, making sure that your mitred corners are perfectly square and nail in place. Complete the frame in the same way with the other 2 side pieces.

8. FIT LIGHTS

Remove the bulbs from your lights and push the bulb holders through the holes from the back. Screw the bulbs in to secure the light string in place. Fix the switch unit in one of the bottom corners at the back of the frame so it is accessible.

PALLET-WOOD BOX FRAME

I love having art on the walls but let's be honest, it can be expensive. Also I find that just hanging a canvas print looks a bit naked and a lot of frames are just boring and traditional. As an alternative to the more usual mitred frame design, with a 45° angle at the corners, why not go for a simple butt joint? In this design I also turn pallet wood on its side, to create extra depth. The result is a box, which means I can display bits and pieces on top and on the shelf, as well as fixing artwork to the back of the frame.

This is a great way to use shorter pieces of pallet wood that aren't long enough for other projects. The rough texture just adds to the interest.

ITEMS TO SOURCE:
• Pallet wood offcuts

1. SELECT YOUR WOOD

Lay out your offcuts to decide which pieces you are going to use for the back. Make the most of any interesting textures in the grain. Cut to length. You do not need to join these pieces together — they will be held in place by the frame.

2. CUT FRAME

Cut the sides for the frame. These should be overlapped all around rather then aiming for symmetrical.

3. DRILL PILOT HOLES

Mark out where you will attach the frame to the back section. Drill pilot holes to prevent the wood splitting.

4. ASSEMBLE FRAME

Nail the first side to one of the back components using ring shank nails. These are commonly used in the production of pallets so are ideal.

5. MAKE SQUARE

Lay the frame down on the bench to make sure it is square and continue to nail the sections together.

6. FINISH AND SAND

Check that the angles are true and sand any rough edges. Finish with wax or leave untreated if you prefer.

7. ADD ARTWORK

Use double-sided tape to fix your chosen image or images in place (that way you can change them easily). The frame is also deep enough to accommodate keepsakes and mementos.

TIP: The box construction of this frame means it can sit on a shelf or be wall-mounted.

LADDER LIGHT

This design is an emotional one for me as the ladder I converted is my late father's, and it even has his name written on the side for added sentimental value. The design will vary slightly depending on the style of ladder, but ultimately you are looking to create something that is beautiful and offers a functional storage solution, as well as incorporating a caged light bulb. With filament bulbs making a huge comeback, it seems such a shame to cover them up with a shade. The caged shade frames the light bulb beautifully and creates some wonderful shadows on the walls.

ITEMS TO SOURCE:
- Old wooden ladder
- Lamp holder and cable
- Metal lampshade cage

1. CUT LADDER

Find a suitable wooden ladder. You can clean it up a bit if you wish, or leave it in its original state, with all evidence of past use proudly on display! Take the ladder apart and retain the tread side and the larger top shelf. I designed this to lean against a wall, so cut the top of the ladder posts at an angle, so that the ladder will sit flat against a wall. The top shelf usually pivots. In order to fix it more solidly you have to cut square notches at the top of the posts into which the shelf will slot.

2. ATTACH STEP

Re-fit the top shelf, insetting it into the notches so that it sticks out horizontally from the frame. Secure the shelf in place using screws, screwing from the back into the ladder post. Drill pilot holes first if you think the wood will split.

3. THREAD LAMP HOLDER

Connect the lamp holder to the cable. Feed the cable through the metal shade and up and over the top shelf. Loop it around one of the cross bars of the ladder to lock it in place. You can also drill holes in the side supports to feed the cable through. Finally, fit the bulb.

FIX TOP SHELF HORIZONTALLY

CABLE LOOPS BACK ON ITSELF TO LOCK FIRMLY

4. THREAD CABLE

TIP: If your metal frame allows easy access you can use a switched lamp holder. If not you can use an inline switch at a convenient place further down the cable, or switch the light on and off at a wall socket.

GLASS SWEET JAR WALL LAMP

This lamp was actually designed for my houseboat as I was desperate to have a wall-mounted shelf near my bed that wasn't taken up entirely by a bedside lamp. The solution? Hang the lamp below the shelf using a gorgeous brown leather upcycled belt. Then the space on top is left clear for me to prop some books or a glass of water. You need a jar with a wide enough opening to allow a bulb fitting to feed through. The wiring is channelled through the shelf itself so there are no ugly wires hanging loose. The jar I found has a ribbed design, so as an added bonus the effect the light creates through its contoured form is stunning.

ITEMS TO SOURCE:
- *Piece of scaffold board*
- *Glass jar*
- *Leather belt*
- *Jubilee clip*
- *Lamp holder and cable*

1. CUT THE CURVE

To form the curved end of the shelf draw around half the base of the sweet jar. Cut this out using a jigsaw.

2. MARK WOOD

Turn the jar upside down and draw around the top, so you have a guide for the position of the slots for the belt.

3. MEASURE AND MARK SLOTS

Measure the width of your belt. Use this measurement to mark the correct width of the slots.

4. DRILL AND CUT SLOTS

Drill a hole at each end of the marked lines then cut between the holes with a jigsaw.

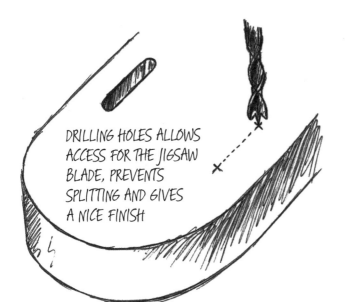

DRILLING HOLES ALLOWS ACCESS FOR THE JIGSAW BLADE, PREVENTS SPLITTING AND GIVES A NICE FINISH

5. DRILL HOLE FOR CABLE

Drill a hole in the end of the shelf that will be attached to the wall for the electrical cable. Make this oversized so you can feed the cable through easily. From underneath, midway between your slots, drill another hole (to the same diameter). Angle it so that it will meet up with your first hole, so you have a passage all the way through the shelf for the cable.

6. THREAD BELT STRAP

Insert the leather belt through the slots, then cut to the desired length with a retractable knife (box cutter).

7. TRIM ENDS

Cut a neat curve on each end.

8. DRILL BELT

Drill a hole in the centre of the semicircle at each end.

9. CONNECT BELT AND CLIP

Drill 2 holes in a metal jubilee clip to align with the holes in the leather belt. Attach the jubilee clip to the belt using a rivet gun. This makes a strong, secure fastening and the shiny rivet also looks great against the brown leather belt.

10. TIGHTEN CLIP

Slide the jubilee clip around the neck of the jar. Use a screwdriver to tighten the clip until it fits snugly around the neck of the jar.

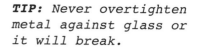

TIP: Never overtighten metal against glass or it will break.

11. THREAD CABLE

Feed the cable through the hole at the back of the shelf and pull through the hole above the jar. Attach the lamp holder and light bulb and suspend it in the jar.

Ask a qualified electrician to hard-wire the light fitting into the lighting circuit.

JELLY MOULD PENDANT LAMPS

These are very simple to make yet beautiful lampshades, constructed using iconic aluminium jelly (jello) moulds. You can pick these up for next to nothing at car boot or yard sales and charity shops (thrift stores) and who could resist their nostalgic charm? If you produce a set of three you can create a real feature above a dining table or a kitchen breakfast bar. If you are lucky enough to find them, maybe you could splash out and use copper moulds? To complete the vintage look you can use old-fashioned braided cloth electrical cable, which is easy to source online.

ITEMS TO SOURCE:
- *Old metal jelly (jello) moulds*
- *Light fitting and cable*
- *Lampshade collar*

1. MARK TOP OF MOULD

Find the centre of the top of the jelly (jello) mould and mark with a pen.

2. PUNCH GUIDE

Create an indent on the mark using a centre punch. This will stop the drill from slipping on the smooth metal.

3. CUT OUT HOLE

Using a hole saw cut a hole slightly larger than the diameter of your lamp holder.

4. FILE SHARP EDGES

Smooth the edges of the hole with a curved file.

5. FIX LAMP HOLDER

Thread the lamp holder through the hole. Use a lampshade collar to keep it in place. Finally, fit the bulb. If you are just replacing the shade you can fit this yourself, but if you are replacing the cable you will need a qualified electrician to do this for you.

TIP: *I really like LED filament bulbs as they not only look beautiful but also don't get hot like traditional filament bulbs.*

ANTLER COAT RACK

Upcycling doesn't have to be limited to just painting and sanding old furniture. You can also follow trends and create the season's must-have items. We have been inundated with antlers and hunting artefacts recently so why not produce some made from reclaimed materials? Once waxed, the natural grain of scaffold boards even resembles the tones and finish of antlers! And the brushed aluminium of the scaffold join gives an industrial edge to the hunting-lodge vibe.

ITEMS TO SOURCE:
* *Offcuts of scaffolding board or similar wood*
* *Scaffold elbow/90° joint*

1. DRAW SHAPES

Mark out the shapes for your antlers and the shield on your wood. Cut out carefully using a jigsaw and sand all the cut edges smooth.

2. FINISH ANTLERS

Wax the antlers to bring out the beauty of the wood. Sand lightly to create highlights in the grain.

3. PAINT SHIELD

Paint the shield in a colour of your choice. Allow to dry.

4. SAND SHIELD

Sand back the paint to reveal some of the wood, especially on the edges, for an attractive distressed look.

5. ADD ELBOW JOINT

Insert both antlers into the scaffold joint. You might need to sand the edges to get it to fit snugly.

6. DRILL FOR FIXING

Drill holes in the shield for screws to pass through in line with the holes in the scaffold joint.

7. SCREW TOGETHER

Place your components face down and screw the shield through the holes in the scaffold joint and into the wood of the antlers. It's now ready to hang on the wall!

TOOLS & TECHNIQUES

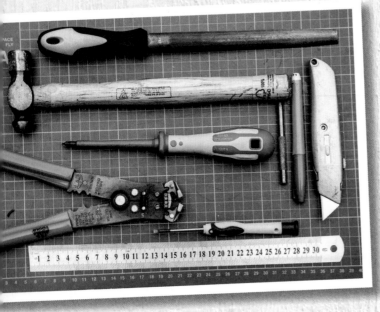

TOOLBOX

HAND TOOLS

Your upcycling toolbox should contain the basics, most of which, no doubt, you will already have:

- Pencil & marker
- Tape measure
- Set square
- Hammer
- Screwdrivers
- Spanners (wrenches)
- Ruler
- Wire strippers
- File
- Retractable knife (box cutter)
- Wood saw
- Clamps

POWER TOOLS

Don't be scared, be respectful! They are big, shiny and noisy. We've all heard the stories of tradesmen who have lost limbs, and in schools and colleges power tools are surrounded by guards, warning signs and yellow lines on the ground that suggest if crossed you'll lose your head.

I actually find that power tools in general are pretty safe, largely because you are likely to be a little apprehensive when using them, which increases your concentration levels and makes you give them the respect they deserve. I have actually injured myself more times using a screwdriver than when using a big power tool.

Always follow basic safety procedures:
- Make sure hair, ties and toggles are tied back and out of the way.
- Never wear gloves with drills as they can catch in the spinning chuck (learned this one the hard way!)

- Switch off the machine with the plug next to you when changing blades etc.
- Always don protective goggles and gloves when cutting or sanding metal.

Once you have respect for these machines and you are safe, you should be able to enjoy achieving great results and be able to manufacture your creations more accurately and quickly.

This is a basic list of power tools and their uses which may come in useful for making the projects in this book:

CORDLESS DRILL - Can be used anywhere (no need to access a socket) for drilling holes, inserting screws and even polishing and sanding with the right attachments.

ELECTRIC SANDERS - Come in various sizes to handle everything from detailed work to heavy-duty stripping. See Sanding, page 133 for a rundown.

ANGLE GRINDER - Generally used for cutting, sanding or polishing metal (see Sanding, page 133.) The thin blade, for example, is great at cutting cast-iron bathtubs, the sanding disc is good for sanding back the cut edges of a shopping trolley and the polishing pad for making aeroplane wings nice and shiny!

MITRE SAW - A spinning circular blade used to cut wood; most cut in at at least one angle but some cut in two.

JIGSAW - Great for cutting intricate shapes. Can be used on most materials with the appropriate blade. No use for straight lines unless you use a guide.

CIRCULAR SAW - A hand-held circular blade, similar to a table saw. Perfect for cutting straight lines but no good for curves or details.

TABLE SAW - As the name suggests this is a circular blade protruding up through a table or workbench. Great for cutting large flat sheets of wood.

RIVET GUN - A simple way of joining two pieces of flat material. Simply drill a hole through both pieces, place a rivet in the hole and pull the trigger.

WELDER - A little more specialist and requires decent safety equipment, but basically joins metal to metal without the need for fixings. Equipment can be expensive and takes a bit of practice but very satisfying once mastered (see also Welding, page 141).

UPCYCLING TRICKS & TECHNIQUES

SALVAGING WOOD

There are lots of different types of wood available to the eagle-eyed scavenger. Pallets are available from most industrial estates as most businesses receive their deliveries on them and have no way of getting rid of them. If you ask nicely the business owner will generally encourage you to take them.

Plywood is also a fairly common timber — to find decent offcuts check skips (dumpsters), building sites and your local dump. A lot of old furniture was made of solid timber and even modern pine furniture is great to work with. The only wood I try to avoid is chipboard as it's not nice to work with, doesn't give a great finish on the edges and contains lots of glue, which isn't great for respiratory issues.

Old telephone poles can be useful, as are scaffold boards, although both of these are becoming more sought after and hence slightly more expensive. Railway sleepers are gorgeous great lumps of timber but beware any nasty chemicals they might have been treated with.

Always think about not only which wood looks best for the project but also what strength you require. Plywood, for example, is extremely strong end on but is quite flexible. Scaffold boards are usually made from wood that is force grown and hence can twist and split a bit. Sometimes, of course, these attributes can lend themselves to your design, such as steam-bending plywood.

SAWING

There are hundreds of different saw styles, but one top tip - go slowly and don't press too hard!

Whether you are using a high-powered circular saw or a junior hacksaw, let the saw do the work. Always use the correct blades for the material you are using and remember when you apply lots of friction to a material you will get flying debris, sharp edges and heat!

HAND SAWS - The blade is usually directional. The teeth cut more when you push and less when you pull. To get started pull the saw gently a couple of times to create a small grove, then you can start gently pushing forward. Try not to limit yourself to the centre of the blade; long slow strokes using the entire blade will make sawing easier and prolong the life of your blade.

MACHINE SAWS - Whether a circular spinning blade, reciprocating blade or a continuous band these saws cut fingers off! Treat them with respect, however, and they are your best friend and will save you hours and create more accurate cuts. When possible try to clamp down anything you are cutting, follow safety instructions and, as with hand sawing, take your time and don't push it.

HOW TO TAKE APART A WOODEN PALLET

While pallets are easy to come by and usually free, you should consider the time it takes to take them apart. Pallets tend to be produced using ring shank nails – the manufacturer doesn't take into account us wanting to take them apart! Ring shank nails are designed to go in and not come out, so even if you are gentle or use a pallet breaker the chances are the nails at the end will split the wood. My approach is to design the item around the length of the pallet wood between the outer nails, which means I can cut the pallet with a circular or hand saw along the outside edges first, then use the length to lever against itself to pull out the centre nails.

MEASURING, CUTTING & MARKING

'Measure twice, cut once' is an old saying but very true. Taking your time measuring and marking out can save you time and money in mistakes.

Tape measures are awesome. Take that bit of metal on the end of the tape. It isn't loose due to shoddy workmanship. The slack allows you to gain a true measurement when you push the metal against a surface (it moves inwards). When you hook it over an item it pulls out by its thickness - genius, huh?

Tape measures also usually have their own width marked on them, so if you're measuring an internal dimension you don't need to bend the tape awkwardly — you simply butt the tape measure body up to the edge and add that width to the reading on the tape.

Another nifty little feature is the hole cut from the metal end: this is designed to hook over a screw head. When working on your own you can temporarily place a screw where you need to measure from so you can get a good steady measurement.

Not sure how intentional this next feature is but I use it all the time: if you are measuring a piece of soft timber you can mark the length without a pencil by simply scoring the metal end onto the wood. This doesn't work as well with metal or hardwood, but still generally leaves a mark and helps you out if working without a pencil.

And did you know the angles between a saw blade and its handle gives you 45° and 90° measurements? Useful to know when you are cutting lengths of timber.

SANDING

Sanding is one of the most common tasks in my workshop and can be strangely therapeutic. I enjoy nothing more than to have the doors open, sun streaming in, music playing and tea brewing while I sand a beautiful piece of timber.

There are lots of different tools that rotate, vibrate and spin in various grit sizes and densities to achieve the desired level of smoothness.

PALM/DETAIL SANDER - This small hand-held tool is perfect for woodwork. Various grits of sandpaper can be fitted. The pad vibrates vigorously, which makes it quite safe to use; however, it can leave marks if you don't use fine enough paper.

ORBITAL SANDER - More vigorous than the smaller detail sander. Removes material a lot quicker but is less controllable.

BELT SANDER — As the name suggests the sandpaper is one continuous belt that revolves. These range from small single-handed tools to much larger bench-mounted machines, but they all remove material rapidly and can leave grooves if not used with care. A selection of grits is available, although I wouldn't recommend using these for very fine work.

ANGLE GRINDER - Typically used for cutting and grinding metal, but can also be used to sand and polish. Sanding discs consist of a series of pieces of sandpaper lapped over each other to form an entire disc.

HAND SANDING - The most primitive yet wonderfully enjoyable method, either holding the sandpaper directly in your hand or wrapping it around a small block of wood or cork. It allows you to be in touch with the material, so better for finer finishing. Also great if you are trying to achieve the distressed look.

With all of these techniques try to sand with the grain and work down through the grits gradually, from rough to smooth.

SANDPAPER — Basic sandpapers come in rough and smooth, but more expensive ones have a number on the back such as 80 or 240. This refers to the number of particles of grit per square inch: the higher the number, the finer the sandpaper and the smoother the finish. To achieve the best results start with a rough paper such as a 40 or 80, work up to a 240, then finish with something as fine as a 600, or wet and dry, which is really smooth, to finish.

DRILLING

Drill bits come in all shapes and sizes and ultimately just spin really fast to make a hole, but choosing the correct one for the job and material is vital, as are condition and sharpness. The main tip for drilling neat holes is to let the drill do the work: apply some pressure, but if you push too hard you will either snap the drill bit, get a wonky hole or just blunt the end.

DRILLING METAL To avoid the tip slipping locate your drill by making a punched indentation first. Start with a small bit and work up through the sizes rather then struggling with a large bit from the start. You can apply a cutting compound to lubricate and cool the metal.

PILOT HOLES When screwing wood together it can split – to make matters worse this usually happens once you've cut all the parts, sanded and waxed them and all that needs doing is one simple little screw! To avoid this, drill a small hole first, roughly the size of the shaft of the screw (not including the thread). This gives the screw somewhere to go while still allowing the thread to bite.

COUNTERSINKING If you are screwing into a soft material sometimes a countersunk screw (see page 140) just pulls into the material. However, in a hard material you need to remove a small inverted cone for the screw head to sit in. Countersunk bits are fairly cheap, make life easier, work better and some are even built into a pilot drill bit.

THERE ARE HUNDREDS OF DRILL BIT STYLES BUT THE MAIN 3 ARE WOOD, METAL AND MASONRY

UPHOLSTERY

Most modern-day upholstery involves three main components: the fabric, foam and a wooden base. The fabric is pulled taught over the foam and stapled into the underside of the wooden base. In order to achieve a smooth, unfolded look you should pull the fabric tight, attaching a staple in the centre of each side first to locate the fabric and ensure any pattern is aligned before working from the centre of an edge back towards the corners.

A few upholstery top tips:

• Cut the fabric larger all the way around your foam by at least 10cm (4in). You can always trim it afterwards.

• Use the correct knife to cut the foam. Most sharp knifes just tear upholstery foam. I like to use a cheap twin blade electric carving knife, but a very sharp hand carving knife can also work well.

• When you apply your first few locating staples fix them at an angle as they might need to come out later. If not you can always tap them in with a hammer.

• Buy a good staple gun. Upholstering is a real pleasure if the equipment you are using is comfortable to use.

• Always consider how you intend fixing any upholstery to the item of furniture. It's easy to build in fixing methods as you go, but it's tricky to retrofit tabs, ties or fixing holes.

GLASS

Every glass merchant is different, but typically if you are after just one piece they won't want the hassle of fancy CAD models, they would much prefer a wooden template. The beauty of this is that you can also work with this on your item to make sure the levels work visually and physically. Use a piece of wood that is a similar thickness and write the requirements on the template, such as thickness, whether clear or sandblasted and whether you want rounded corners so they are child friendly. I always order toughened glass so if there is an accident it won't splinter, and you should also state how you would like the edges finished – I usually opt for polished to ensure they are smooth.

If in doubt which thickness to use take advice from the glass merchant. It depends on the project, but I usually choose 12mm ($^1/_2$in) for a small well-supported coffee table all the way up to 18mm ($^3/_4$in) thick for a larger desk.

Always consider where and how the glass is to be supported. Remember it doesn't always need to be stuck down or secured as it will probably be heavy enough to just rest on some rubber pads to stop it slipping.

ELECTRIC WIRING

People are wary of wiring, but a lot of it is common sense and securing copper wires into screw terminals. That said, you must treat electricity with respect and if in doubt, or if you want to wire a light fitting into the main circuit rather than create a free-standing plug-in light fitting, consult an expert.

Most plugs, switches and lamp holders come with instructions and as long as you take your time and ensure the wires are securely attached in the correct locations you should be fine.

The real issues as a designer are how you actually fit the cables, switches and lamp holders, ensuring bulbs are secured so the weight isn't hanging on the cable, and issues such as heat ventilation and how to change the bulb.

Style-wise, filament bulbs are very popular right now and a lot of designers are using traditional cables with bright and beautiful fabric finishes to add a touch of vintage class to their designs.

When working on metal items you must make sure your cables are not exposed to sharp edges, which may in time cut through. To avoid this you can drill an oversized hole in thin metal areas and insert a rubber grommet. You might also need to earth any metal lamps, depending on your country's electrical system.

FINISHES

Different materials react differently to paints and coating. Some require preparation and some don't. Here is a list of some of the most commonly used finishes and when they are suitable:

PAINTING WOOD WITH A BRUSH is the easiest and cheapest form of painting. If using normal emulsion on wood you need to ensure the surface is keyed with sandpaper to make it less glossy, then cleaned thoroughly. You will then probably need to apply two coats of paint following the grain. As with all painting a few thin layers are better than one thick layer.

PAINTING METAL WITH A BRUSH I find to be trickier than painting wood as it's not as forgiving. There are metal paints on the market that claim to be one coat, but I struggle to get a good finish if I'm honest, and brush strokes aren't as aesthetically acceptable on metal as they are on wood.

PAINTING WOOD WITH SPRAY CANS takes practice and you need a mask and a well-ventilated area to work in, but this method avoids brush strokes. I usually prime the items first.

PAINTING METAL WITH SPRAY CANS works much better than brushing in my opinion, but you must really prepare the surface well. Ideally you should shot-blast the metal first to make sure it's really clean, degrease it, then spray. You are into professional territory here, and for a little extra cost you could probably get your work professionally wet-painted or powder-coated.

SPRAY-PAINTING METAL PROFESSIONALLY can be expensive but worth it. Much of the time is spent masking the item and changing colours in the spray gun, so consider how many colours you want.

POWDER COATING is the most durable of finishes on metal. As the name suggests, an electrostatic gun imparts a layer of powder to a metal object, imbuing it with a positive electric charge so it adheres to the metal. I always powder coat metal products where possible, as it's a great finish that lasts for ages and withstands chips and scratches.

ELECTROPLATING is the finish you find on shopping trolleys (carts). It's very hard wearing as it almost becomes part of the metal through applying electrodes in a tank. You are slightly limited in terms of colours, although more choice is becoming available.

CHALKY FINISH PAINTS have been around for years, but with the recent trend for painted furniture lots of manufacturers have launched their own versions. Chalky finish paint contains a number of ingredients, but the main ones are resins to help the paint stick to the surface and chalk to give it a textural finish. The benefits are that it sticks well to glossy unsanded surfaces, usually requires only one coat and looks lovely when lightly sanded and distressed. I usually apply a clear wax over the top of chalk paint to seal it.

WAXING was for years limited to light or dark brown. Recently, however, we have seen the launch of a number of lovely waxes from taupe, grey and cream to glittery gold and silver. I love using wax: it doesn't completely cover the origins of the wood, nourishes and even smells great! Apply wax with either wire wool to get in the grain or a soft lint-free cloth for an even light coating.

DISTRESSING means many things to many people, but I personally see it as giving a product an aged look. Some see this as faking a product's history, but you can do it subtly and just gently add to the look. When we distress dining tables made from scaffold boards we sand the boards with a rough grit sandpaper, paint them a base colour then, using a fine grit sand over the paint, deliberately catch proud details and edges that would naturally get worn most over the years. Once again, use a clear wax to coat the entire thing.

DRY BRUSHING is a new technique to me that I've only just started experimenting with. It's basically a much quicker and easier way of creating the distressed look. You can either start with a painted item or paint it a neutral base coat. Then, as the name suggests, you apply a contrasting colour to your brush and wipe it with a cloth until the paint is almost entirely removed. You then lightly scrub this over the item, deliberately catching the details and raised areas. On flat surfaces it can be tricky to make this look authentic, but we have found going vertical and horizontal works best — this takes some practice but looks great once you've mastered it and you can achieve brilliant results very quickly.

LACQUERING is a useful technique if you want the finish to be protected without the traditional look of varnishing. The paintwork on a car, for example, is sanded back with very fine paper before several layers of lacquer are applied.

FIXING & JOINING

Nuts, bolts, two-part resins, Phillips, pozi, flat-head screws — the terminology is endless so here is a quick insight into each and how they can be used.

BOLTS are the long thin bits, nuts are the smaller fatter bits that thread onto the bolt — so many people still get this confused! They come in basic metric or imperial sizes — an 8mm diameter bolt is called an M8. You then specify the length in mm. As standard, bolts have a hexagonal-shaped head that is tightened using either spanners or socket sets. The pitch refers to the distance between each thread. The majority of threads are standard pitch, but you occasionally find fine-pitch threads on items such as electrical lighting and spark plugs.

NUTS are the smaller hexagonal bits that thread onto the bolt. They are usually just described by the M number as outlined above. You usually fit a washer to a bolt before the nut to ensure it spins on the washer rather than scratching the surface of the material. If you want a nut to stay fixed for a long time use a nut with a nylon sleeve or tighten two nuts against each other.

HEX HEAD is the standard bolt head shape.

BUTTON-HEAD BOLTS have a much prettier domed head with a recessed small hexagonal hole into which you place an Allen key (hex wrench) to tighten.

They are similar to standard bolts, but more ornate and more expensive. You cannot achieve quite the same level of tightness or torque with these compared with standard hex-head bolts.

COACH BOLTS have a domed head but no recess; this may appear strange as it looks like it's impossible to hold the head as you tighten and slacken the bolt. The secret is a square shank directly under the head which, as you tighten, digs into a soft material such as wood, stopping it from spinning as you tighten.

NYLOCK NUTS are standard-looking hexagonal nuts but with a nylon insert that binds to the thread as you tighten it. They are used when you don't want the thread to be removed or work loose.

DOMED NUTS work like a standard nut but they have a domed top rather than a flat one so they can only be used on the end of a thread. They are more ornate, designed to be on view, and give increased safety as the bolt thread or sharp end is not exposed.

WASHERS are generally placed between the bolt head and the surface as well as the nut and the surface. These simple rings, which prevent the nut or bolt head scratching the surface, can be a variety of materials, but typically are metal, rubber, nylon or cork.

A single slot in the screw head means the screwdriver can slip and damage the surface and they are not very easy to use with an electric screwdriver as they don't self-centre. But they do look lovely if you line a number of them up all facing the same way!

SELF-TAPPING SCREWS, as the name suggests, create their own hole in the material, though you can still create a pilot hole to ensure they drive in straight. These are typically used for fast woodwork projects. The screw itself is usually countersunk with a pointed end and sometimes a serrated thread to make it cut into the material more easily.

PHILLIPS (CROSSHEAD) SCREWS have a pointed recess in the head with 4 points of contact to prevent the screwdriver slipping, as it can on flat-head screws.

POZI DRIVE SCREWS are similar to the Phillips screw but with four smaller indents between the original four so there are even more points of contact – great when using electric screwdrivers.

COUNTERSUNK SCREWS are used when you wish the screw head to sit flush with the surface of a material. They naturally pull into a soft material such as timber but require a drilled countersunk hole to be made in hard materials.

FLAT-HEAD SCREWS are much more traditional and purists love the look, but they are less easy to use.

MACHINE SCREWS are effectively bolts with a screw head. The shaft has a set diameter with a pitched thread.

METAL GLUE is not a fixing method I tend to use — I prefer to attach metal by welding or bolting — but some modern cars are actually glued together! This is not very environmentally friendly if you are joining different metals as they cannot be easily separated and recycled at the end of their life.

TWO-PART GLUE, more commonly known as epoxy glue, usually contains two separate liquids: an epoxy resin and a hardener. When the two components mix they create a chemical reaction that sets very hard. These glues cure quickly and create a really strong bond between most materials.

WOOD GLUE, such as PVA, is great for wood joints and fixing biscuit joints etc. (see below), and strong when used in conjunction with a mechanical fixing. Gluing and screwing is commonly used in furniture making, for example.

BISCUITING If you are gluing two pieces of timber end on, glue probably won't hold and a screw might not be long enough. If you cut a groove out of the touching faces of both components you can then insert a little wooden oval biscuit, which when glued expands and holds the two pieces of timber together.

RIVETING Commonly found in aviation, rivets are a fixing that cannot be undone. Basically you drill a hole through two pieces of material then place a rivet through. When you apply a rivet gun to the rivet you compress it, which crumples and squeezes the components together to lock them fixed.

MIG WELDING is the most common form of welding. You place two items of metal next to each other, hold the mig welding torch at an angle against them and pull the trigger. It self-feeds a wire that melts due to an electric arc; this fuses the two metal items together to create a permanent fixing. This technique is quite noisy and not too pretty but is a very effective way to join metal.

TIG WELDING is similar to mig welding, but you feed the wire with your other hand. It is trickier but much less aggressive and neater once mastered.

SPOT WELDING An electric current is passed through the pieces of metal from an electrode, which clamps around the metal in one single spot. This is how most cars are currently produced.

SOLDERING is typically used to join circuit boards to electronic components. A hand-held soldering iron has a tip that gets very hot. You position this tip next to the wire you wish to solder, you then feed a flux into the joint, which melts and fuses the items together.

WOODWORKING JOINTS – THE BASICS

I'm not a carpenter or cabinet-maker but as a well-rounded designer you need to at least be aware of various joints in all materials. In most industries manufacturers try to hide joints; in woodwork they embrace and enjoy them!

BUTT JOINTS The most simple of joints: just butt one end of the timber up to the flat face of the other, and fix with nails, screws or glue and screws for added strength. This relies on the fixing as the wood is not interlinked.

45° MITRED JOINTS Think of a picture frame: to create a 90° angle you cut both pieces of wood at 45°.

DOVETAIL JOINT A more traditional joining method, which can be seen on such items as old sets of drawers. You remove sections from both joining materials so they interlock together. Each section is shaped like a dovetail, hence the name.

MORTISE AND TENON JOINTS A very old method of joining, typically at 90°. It is simply a slotted hole in one piece (the mortise) and a tongue (the tenon) on the other. It is quite simple and very strong, and usually used in buildings and larger designs.

SOURCES

So you've now hopefully been inspired and have loads of lovely upcycling ideas, the tools are looked out and dusted down but where do you find all the materials?

Well, there isn't to my knowledge a one-stop shop for upcycling materials unfortunately, so you're going to have to put in a little bit of work.

With the internet at our disposal you no longer need to go scavenging round car boots and antique markets, but let's be honest, this can be amazing fun and you can pick up some real gems and bargains.

I enjoy nothing more than getting up early on a Sunday morning and attending an auction or antique market. I think it's the thrill of finding a really beautiful item that only you see potential in that excites me the most.

Finding the more structural materials such as scaffold boards and pallets requires a somewhat different approach. If you pay your local industrial estate a visit you will find that a lot of businesses are more than happy to give you pallets for free. They get a lot of their materials delivered on pallets and usually don't have much of a need for them afterwards.

Scaffold companies tend to trim their boards down when the ends get split until they become too short to use on site, then they get thrown in a pile. If you are prepared to sort through them you will likely get some lovely weathered boards for free — or a small donation! The scaffold poles have a very similar life expectancy to the boards. But they also often get used on site for cable management, and then get run over by the ginormous trucks and bent. Once bent the poles are unuseable as scaffolding, so get thrown next to the boards on the scrap pile.

Another fantastic source for good-quality furniture are charity shops, second-hand shops, thrift stores and furniture banks. All of these places are jam-packed with decent furniture made from solid timber that is just a bit unloved as it doesn't have the right paint job or isn't upholstered in this season's fabric.

Searching online for your upcycling materials couldn't be easier: we have auction sites, classified adverts and even local swap meets. There are forums and hubs discussing materials, techniques and even members offering items for free.

There has never been a better time to get upcycling. Just remember to move quickly as there are lots of like-minded people out there just waiting to grab those bargains!

ACKNOWLEDGEMENTS

So how do you write this bit without sounding all gushing and clichéd?

First and foremost I would like to thank my mum and dad. They gave me the confidence and self-belief to constantly venture out of my comfort zone and believe I could achieve anything and everything I wanted.

My father passed away shortly after my success in the Dragons' Den, but I like to think he was satisfied I was going to be okay, able to look after my mother and uphold the family name. My dad spent countless hours teaching me his DIY skills, passing on his OCD ways and ensuring I completed every task as efficiently and carefully as possible (including how to eat an ice cream without it dripping!) My mother is an absolute rock and the most patient woman in the world to put up with my dad and me.

I would also like to thank and apologize to my partners, past and present, friends and family for all the stressful times, highs, lows and nearlys!

I've cried publicly several times talking about my high school design teacher Mr John Bonson. He focused my attention, captured my imagination and it kind of helped that we both loved rugby! I found sanctuary in the design department and in a world of academia I found success and reward. KISS - Keep It Simple Stupid — was his design mantra.

A huge thank you to the talented publishing team at Jacqui Small who have spent countless hours sifting through my ramblings and who have made me look handsome in photographs. And of course to Simon Brown for his simply stunning photography.

Finally to the slave driver and absolute machine that is my agent Debbie Catchpole. I approached her a couple of years ago asking for as much work as she could throw at me, and boy can that woman throw! Debbie and her incredible team manage my life, send flowers, book train tickets and arrange flights like a crack commando team.

I feel truly blessed and love what I do. Hopefully I can inspire a few others along the way.

Dad, this is for you xxx